Koprince Law LLC GovCon Handbooks

Volume 1: Joint Ventures

A Comprehensive Guide to Government Contracts Joint Ventures – In Plain English

Steven J. Koprince & Candace M. Shields

Nothing contained in this book is to be considered as the rendering of legal advice for specific cases, and readers are responsible for obtaining such advice from their own legal counsel. This book is intended for educational and information purposes only. Although the authors strive to present accurate information, the information provided in this book is not guaranteed to be accurate, complete, or up-to-date. Buying or reading this book does not establish an attorney-client relationship with the authors and/or Koprince Law LLC.

© *2018 Steven J. Koprince*
All rights reserved
Published January 2018

Contents

INTRODUCTION 1
    ABOUT THIS HANDBOOK 2
    ABOUT THIS SERIES 4
    TWO BRIEF DISCLAIMERS 4
    LET'S GET STARTED 5

PART I – JOINT VENTURES 101 6
    TO JV OR NOT TO JV: THAT IS THE QUESTION 9
    JV LEGAL REQUIREMENTS: THE BIG PICTURE 12

PART II – JOINT VENTURE ELIGIBILITY 17
    CONTRACTS, NOT ORDERS 18
    SIZES OF JOINT VENTURE PARTNERS 22
    SOCIOECONOMIC STATUS 29
    THE "THREE-IN-TWO" RULE 32

PART III – JOINT VENTURE FORMATION 40
    WRITING/OWN NAME 40
    REGISTERED IN SAM 43
    UNPOPULATED SEPARATE LEGAL ENTITY 44
    MANDATORY JOINT VENTURE PROVISIONS 46
    DON'T UNDERMINE MANDATORY JOINT VENTURE PROVISIONS 58
    AMENDING JOINT VENTURES 60
    PRIOR APPROVAL OF JOINT VENTURES 62

PART IV – JOINT VENTURE PERFORMANCE 67
    PERFORMANCE OF WORK REQUIREMENTS 67
    JOINT VENTURE INTERNAL WORK SHARE REQUIREMENTS 70
    TYPE OF WORK PERFORMED 74

CERTIFICATIONS AND REPORTS 74
INSPECTION OF RECORDS 77
JV ACRONYM LIST 78
BIOS 85

INTRODUCTION

For small companies, federal government contracting can be big business. The federal government spends approximately $500 billion annually to buy goods and services from contractors. Thanks to special rules requiring agencies to award contracts to small businesses, about a quarter of those procurement dollars go to small companies. Contracting with the government can be lucrative—but if you don't know the key rules and regulations, it can also be risky.

That's the case when it comes to joint ventures. In recent years, joint venturing has become more and more popular as small businesses seek ways to more effectively compete on larger and more complex acquisitions. The SBA has spurred the increased interest in joint venturing by enacting the All Small Mentor-Protégé Program, which allows all small businesses to joint venture with large mentors. At the same time, the SBA amended its rules to allow small businesses to more easily joint venture with one another.

So far, so good. But just because joint venturing is more widely available doesn't mean that it comes without red tape. When you joint venture for a federal government contract opportunity, you sign up for a host of rules and regulations. Get it wrong, and you could be on the wrong end of a successful protest—or worse.

That's where this Handbook comes in.

ABOUT THIS HANDBOOK

If you've ever searched online for books about federal contracting, you'll see one theme repeated over and over (and over some more): winning. The literary market is overflowing with tomes from authors purporting to tell business owners how to win federal government contracts.

 And who doesn't like winning? Capturing government business is exciting. Compliance, not so much. Search the same databases for books on government contracting compliance, and you'll find a book one of us wrote in 2012 called *The Small-Business Guide to Government Contracts*. And not much else, unless you count hard copies of the FAR itself.

But winning isn't much good if you don't do it right. With that in mind, this Handbook covers government contracts joint ventures from end-to-end: from an initial "Joint Venture 101" through eligibility, formation, and performance of contracts.

This Handbook is written in layman's terms (not "legalese") and uses easy-to-understand terms and examples to explain many of the most important rules small businesses must follow to remain in Uncle Sam's good graces.

Each of the four parts includes several features to help you better understand and apply the rules:

- **Examples**. Key concepts are developed in examples, so that you can see how a rule might apply in the real world. Some examples are loosely based on real-life judicial and administrative decisions; others spring from our fertile imaginations.

- **Check It Out: The Regulations**. If you want to read the rules themselves, each part includes a section telling you where to look. Simply plug in the regulatory citation to your favorite Internet search engine, and you should have no trouble finding the regulation.

- **Myths vs. Realities**. We spend a lot of time talking to government contractors. In these conversations, we hear some of the same joint venture misconceptions repeated over and over. After the Discovery Channel rejected our pitch for a spin-off TV series ("Mythbusters: Government Contracts Law"), we've pieced together our shattered egos and attempted to debunk these myths in this Handbook, instead.

ABOUT THIS SERIES

This Handbook is the first in a series that we and our colleagues will publish. Future editions, like this one, will cover government contracts topics in-depth. If you like this Handbook, please keep your eyes peeled for others in the series.

As each Handbook is published, we'll alert you on our blog, *SmallGovCon* (smallgovcon.com). We've been writing *SmallGovCon* since 2012, and we're at 1,100 posts and counting. *SmallGovCon* is written much like this book: a lot of information, a minimum of legalese, and the occasional bad joke. For those who don't want to click on a legal blog every day, we offer a free electronic monthly newsletter with a roundup of many of our most popular posts. To receive the newsletter, just visit the website and click "Sign up for SmallGovCon email updates" on the right-hand side.

TWO BRIEF DISCLAIMERS

Because this book is, in fact, written by lawyers, and because we lawyers are a cautious bunch by nature, we'll pause here for two important disclaimers.

First, as the text at the front boldly states, this Handbook is intended for your educational use only. It does not constitute legal advice about any specific situation you may face. Reading it (even if you read it very carefully and dog-ear your favorite pages) does not create an attorney-client relationship. Put another way, unless you have signed an engagement letter with our law firm, we are not your lawyers.

Second, like most things in life, the government contracting rules sometimes change. This Handbook reflects the rules as they were in early 2018. Depending on when you're reading this book, most of the rules are probably still the same. But keep an eye on trade publications and blogs (like *SmallGovCon*), and keep your ears open for news that a rule has changed. If you're not sure whether a regulation is still effective, look it up.

LET'S GET STARTED

Alright, that's enough disclaiming for one book, don't you think? Kick off your shoes, lean back, and let's discuss what you need to know to form a compliant government contracts joint venture.

PART I – JOINT VENTURES 101

So, you think you might want to form a joint venture to pursue a federal government contract. That might be a good idea. But first things first: what the heck is a government contracts joint venture, anyway?

The FAR is thousands of pages long in print form, but nevertheless does no favors to small businesses when it comes to answering this question. Instead of providing detailed guidance on joint venturing, the FAR lumps prime/subcontractor teams and joint ventures together under the heading "Contractor Team Arrangements," and pretty much leaves it at that.

The SBA's regulations, on the other hand, have a bit more to say:

> *A joint venture is an association of individuals and/or concerns with interests in any degree or proportion consorting to engage in and carry out no more than three specific or limited-purpose business ventures for joint profit over a two-year period, for which purpose they combine their efforts, property,*

money, skill or knowledge, but not on a continuing or permanent basis for conducting business generally.[1]

Whew. That's quite the lengthy sentence. We'll get back to the important pieces of this definition shortly, but for now, it may be easiest to describe a joint venture by comparing a joint venture to a standard prime/subcontractor teaming relationship.

The easiest way to differentiate between a prime/subcontractor team and a joint venture is to ask: *who is the prime contractor?* In a prime/subcontractor team, only one company—the prime—is the prime contractor. With a joint venture, however, the joint venture itself is the prime contractor, and the joint venture's members are collectively responsible for the joint venture's performance. In other words, a joint venture is a vehicle under which two or more companies can share the benefits and obligations of serving as the prime contractor on a government contract.

With this important conceptual distinction in mind, the key differences between prime/subcontractor teams and joint ventures are all rather logical.

---

[1] 13 C.F.R. § 121.103(h).

Characteristic	Prime/Subcontractor Team	Joint Venture
Government Relationship	Only prime has a direct contractual relationship with the government	All parties (through JV) have a direct contractual relationship with the government
Legal Form	Parties do not form new legal entity	Parties typically form a separate formal legal entity (e.g., LLC)
Scope of Work	Subcontractor responsible for limited subset of prime contract scope of work	Both parties legally responsible for entire prime contract scope of work
Payment	Subcontractor ordinarily paid on a pre-determined basis (e.g., fixed fee)	Parties ordinarily split profits (and losses) from prime contract
Small Business Set-Aside Eligibility	Only prime contractor must be eligible small business (but team must comply with subcontracting limits and ostensible subcontractor rule)	Both parties must be eligible small businesses (except in SBA-approved mentor-protégé relationship)

TO JV OR NOT TO JV: THAT IS THE QUESTION

Now that you've got your arms around the key differences between a prime/subcontractor team and a joint venture, which format do you choose?

While the decision whether to pursue a prime/subcontractor team or joint venture must be made on a case-by-case basis, there are often good reasons to consider a joint venture:

- *Larger Work Share.* As we'll see, a "Partner Venturer" (that is, the venturer that is not the lead) can perform up to 60 percent of the joint venture's work—or more, in some cases. Depending on the circumstances, this may be more work than the same company could perform as a subcontractor.

- *Past Performance/Experience.* The SBA's regulations require a contracting officer to consider the past performance and experience of all joint venture members. In contrast, contrary to common misconception, neither the SBA's regulations nor the FAR require contracting officers to consider the past performance and experience of subcontractors (although contracting officers often do so, anyway).[2]

---

[2] For negotiated procurements, FAR 15.305(a)(2)(iii) says that the evaluation "should take into account . . . subcontractors that will perform major or critical aspects of the requirement." But "should" is not the same as "must."

- *No Termination.* A prime contractor typically has the right to terminate its subcontractor. Sometimes, primes even enjoy the right to terminate their subcontractors for convenience, that is, even when the subcontractor hasn't defaulted. From the sub's perspective, this ain't good. In contrast, a joint venture partner typically is an equity owner in a business—and ordinarily, one equity owner cannot terminate another.
- *Avoid Ostensible Subcontractor Affiliation.* When a large business will play an important subcontracting role on a set-aside contract, there may be a risk of ostensible subcontractor affiliation—which would cause the prime/subcontractor team to be ineligible.[3] Since a joint venture partner isn't a subcontractor, the ostensible subcontractor rule doesn't apply to the relationship between joint venturers—unless, of course, a joint venture partner is also serving as a subcontractor. (However, as we'll discuss, a large business can only be a joint venture partner for a set-aside acquisition under the SBA's mentor-protégé programs).

Of course, there are some downsides to the joint venture, as well:

---

[3] The ostensible subcontractor rule is found at 13 C.F.R. § 121.103(h)(4), and has been interpreted in hundreds of SBA Office of Hearings and Appeals cases over the years. We'll discuss this rule at length in a future GovCon Handbook.

- *Size Requirements.* If one of the partners is a large business, a joint venture might not be doable for set-aside contracts—unless the parties have an SBA-approved mentor-protégé agreement in place.
- *Paperwork.* When you create a joint venture, you are setting up a new legal entity. And that means paperwork: filings with Secretaries of State (usually), joint venture agreements, operating agreements, and so on. Even after the joint venture is formed, there are mandatory SBA reports to file.
- *Red Tape.* All joint ventures must register in every contractor's favorite database: the System for Award Management, or SAM. And some JVs require prior approval by the SBA or the U.S. Department of Veterans Affairs.
- *Cost.* It typically will cost more to form a joint venture than a prime/subcontractor team. There may be state filing fees to establish a new entity, legal fees associated with a joint venture agreement and other internal documentation, bank fees to set up an operating account, and so on. A prime/subcontractor team avoids most of these costs—although legal fees associated with a good teaming agreement and subcontract are still a wise investment.
- *You're Stuck with Those Guys.* The downside of "no termination," is, well, no termination. Barring something unusual like a bankruptcy filing, you're likely stuck with

your joint venture partner for the life of the contract—for better or for worse.

- *Less Work for Construction Subcontractors.* Oddly, in the construction industry, a company ordinarily can perform more work as a subcontractor than it can as a joint venture partner.

JV LEGAL REQUIREMENTS: THE BIG PICTURE

So you want to form your first government contracts joint venture. Now what? Let's break down the process into three phases: the *qualification* phase, the *formation* stage, and the *performance* stage.

In the *qualification* phase, the parties determine whether they are eligible to pursue a set-aside solicitation as joint venturers. This phase includes:

- *Size Eligibility.* The joint venture must qualify as a small business. This can be done the "old fashioned" way (both joint venturers are small businesses). Alternatively, a joint venture between an SBA-approved mentor and protégé may qualify even if the mentor is large.
- *"Three-in-Two."* Ah, the infamous (and some[4] might say, ridiculous) three-in-two rule. As a corollary to size eligibility, a joint venture entity should not bid new

---

[4] Us.

contracts more than two years after it is awarded its first contract. Also, the joint venture should stop bidding when it receives its third award within a two-year period after the first win.
- *Socioeconomic Eligibility.* To pursue an 8(a), SDVOSB, HUBZone or WOSB contract, at least one of the joint venture partners must have the requisite certification or self-certification.

Next up is the *formation* stage: the nuts and bolts of creating the joint venture. Here's what's involved in this second phase:
- *Determine Legal Relationship.* Will the joint venture be formed as a "separate legal entity" (typically a limited liability company) or as an informal partnership?
- *Populated versus unpopulated.* Will the joint venture have its own employees (populated) or perform its worth through its members (unpopulated)? As we'll see, a recent SBA change answers (mostly anyway) this question.
- *Secretary of State Filing.* If the joint venture will be an LLC or other separate legal entity, it must be formally organized by filing with an appropriate state Secretary of State or similar official.
- *SAM (and Related Fun).* Regardless of whether it is an LLC or informal partnership, the joint venture must register in SAM. This, of course, means that it also needs an EIN, DUNS, and CAGE code. Fun!

- *Mentor-Protégé Agreement.* If one of the joint venturers is a large business, the parties must execute a mentor-protégé agreement—and get SBA's approval.
- *Joint Venture Agreement.* All joint ventures for set-aside contracts must adopt written joint venture agreements. If the joint venture will pursue a socioeconomic set-aside (8(a), SDVOSB, HUBZone or WOSB), the joint venture agreement must contain many mandatory provisions set forth by SBA regulations. The same goes if the joint venture is relying upon the mentor-protégé exception from affiliation to qualify for a small business set-aside contract.
- *Operating Agreement.* If the joint venture is formed as an LLC, the parties often elect to adopt an LLC operating agreement, which supplements the joint venture agreement. Operating agreements ordinarily aren't required, but can be a very good idea from a corporate governance perspective.
- *Prior Approval.* If the joint venture will pursue an 8(a) contract or a VA SDVOSB/VOSB[5] contract, the joint venture must obtain the prior approval of the SBA or VA, as appropriate.

---

[5] Just a reminder: if you're confused about any of these acronyms, our handy-dandy list of definitions is at the back of this Handbook.

Finally, we get to the *performance* stage. The joint venture has been awarded a contract, and the parties are performing contract work. This third stage involves:

- *Limitations on Subcontracting.* The joint venture, as the prime contractor, must abide by the applicable limitations on subcontracting.
- *Internal Work Split.* In many cases, the joint venture must also abide by certain floors and ceilings on how work is split between the joint venture members.
- *Recordkeeping.* If the joint venture is subject to one of the "mandatory joint venture terms" requirements, the parties must maintain the joint venture's records in a certain fashion.
- *Statements and Certifications.* The parties must provide certain statements and certifications to the SBA and agency Contracting Officer during performance.

So, there you have it: Joint Ventures 101. Now it's time to get deep into the regulatory weeds. Grab a glass of your favorite beverage[6] and turn the page to Part II, where we'll talk all about joint venture eligibility.

---

[6] May we suggest a pinot noir?

> **CHECK IT OUT: REGULATIONS DISCUSSED IN THIS PART**
>
> FAR 15.305(a)(2) (consideration of past performance)
>
> 13 C.F.R. § 121.103(h) (SBA's definition of joint venture)
>
> 13 C.F.R. § 121.103(h)(4) (ostensible subcontractor rule)
>
> 13 C.F.R. § 124.513 (8(a) joint ventures)
>
> 13 C.F.R. § 125.8 (small business joint ventures)
>
> 13 C.F.R. § 125.18 (SDVOSB & VOSB joint ventures)
>
> 13 C.F.R. § 126.616 (HUBZone Joint Ventures)
>
> 13 C.F.R. § 127.506 (WOSB & EDWOSB Joint Ventures)

PART II – JOINT VENTURE ELIGIBILITY

Okay, class. Joint Venture 101 is over. Now it's time for the advanced stuff. To kick it off, Part II of this GovCon Handbook delves into when a joint venture is (and is not) eligible for a set-aside contract.

To qualify for award of a set-aside contract, a joint venture must satisfy three threshold eligibility requirements:

- *Size.* The joint venture must (one way or another) qualify as a small business under the NAICS code assigned to the government solicitation.[7]
- *Socioeconomic Status.* If the solicitation is set-aside for one of the four major socioeconomic subcategories (8(a), SDVOSB/VOSB, HUBZone, or WOSB/EDWOSB), at least one of the members must have the "right" certification.

---

[7] Most federal solicitations are designated with a single NAICS code and single corresponding size standard. The solicitation should identify the size standard, but if not, check the SBA's size standards table: https://www.sba.gov/sites/default/files/files/Size_Standards_Table.pdf. Figuring out whether a company is a small business is a surprisingly complex subject beyond the scope of this Handbook. But fear not: we'll dive into the SBA's size and affiliation rules in a future edition. Keep your eyes peeled.

- *Qualification as a Joint Venture.* If the joint venture doesn't comply with the SBA's "three-in-two" rule, the SBA may not believe that the entity is a joint venture in the first place. While violation of the three-in-two rule doesn't necessarily preclude the joint venture from being awarded a set-aside contract, it can lead to a big problem: affiliation.

All this sounds relatively straightforward, but this is federal government contracting we're talking about—things are rarely as easy as they first appear.

CONTRACTS, NOT ORDERS

Before we get started with the three main eligibility requirements, let's back up and talk about what solicitations a joint venture can bid on in the first place.

In the vast, wild wonderland of federal government contracting, agencies procure goods and services using a variety of vehicles. Some of these vehicles are stand-alone contracts; others are master agreements that allow goods and services to be procured by way of orders issued to holders of those master agreements.

These master agreements come in many flavors, each with its own fun[8] acronym: GWAC (government-wide acquisition

---

[8] The government must think acronyms are fun; otherwise, why would they have so many?

contract), IDIQ (indefinite delivery, indefinite quantity), MAC (multiple award contract), BPA (blanket purchase agreement), FSS (Federal Supply Schedule), and so on. When an agency buys goods or services using an order under a master agreement, only holders of the master agreement are eligible.

The previous paragraphs are a gross oversimplification of a very complex topic, but for our purpose (which is, after all, joint ventures), a gross oversimplification ought to do the trick. The key takeaway: when a company is awarded a master agreement, it ordinarily cannot use a joint venture to compete for task orders under that agreement because the joint venture doesn't hold the master agreement.

> **EXAMPLE**
> Green Eggs, LLC is awarded a CIO-SP3[9] small business IDIQ contract. The Department of Health and Human Services issues a task order solicitation limited to CIO-SP3 SB contract holders. Green Eggs would like to bid, but is concerned that its corporate experience won't satisfy DHS's requirements. Green Eggs forms a joint venture with Hamilton Services, Inc.
> The joint venture, Green Eggs 'n' Hamilton, submits a proposal for the task order solicitation.

---

[9] "Chief Information Officer – Solutions and Partners 3." Yep, the individual master agreements themselves are often acronym-based, too.

> **Result:** Green Eggs 'n' Hamilton isn't a CIO-SP3 contract holder. Barring a novation[10], the joint venture isn't eligible to bid on orders issued under the CIO-SP3 contract.

That isn't to say that a joint venture cannot win an IDIQ contract like CIO-SP3 SB—in most cases, joint ventures are eligible to bid on these contracts. If a joint venture wins an IDIQ contract, it is, of course, eligible for orders under that IDIQ.

As is the case with other master agreements, contractors holding so-called "Schedule" contracts with the General Services Administration cannot form a traditional joint venture to sell goods or services under those Schedule contracts. However, the GSA *does* allow Schedule contractors to form GSA "Contractor Team Arrangements," or CTAs. And these CTAs, in turn, look a heck of a lot like traditional joint ventures.

As of this writing, the GSA's policy on CTAs remains "Interim" and can be found on the GSA's website. The GSA says that it is working with the SBA to "provide further clarity around the use of CTAs and anticipates issuing final guidance in the future." How long in the future is anyone's guess; the interim policy has been in place for quite some time.

---

[10] A novation is the transfer of a government contract from one entity to another. A novation requires the government's permission. See FAR 42.1204 for the rules governing novations.

Under a GSA CTA, two Schedule contractors can team up to provide a joint proposal for a competitive order. But a GSA CTA is not a mechanism for one contractor to "use" another contractor's Schedule.

Under a GSA CTA, all CTA members must hold a GSA Schedule contract. Period. A GSA CTA cannot be formed between a company that holds a Schedule contract and a company that does not.

> **EXAMPLE**
>
> MaryME IT obtains a GSA IT Schedule 70 contract. After obtaining her Schedule 70 contract, Mary identifies a State Department requirement for IT helpdesk services. The State Department will procure its requirement through a solicitation open only to Schedule 70 vendors. Mary would like to form a GSA CTA with her favorite partner, NowTech, Inc. NowTech does not hold a GSA Schedule contract.
>
> **Result:** MaryME IT and NowTech cannot form a GSA CTA for the State Department requirement because NowTech does not hold a Schedule 70 contract.

There you have it. If you're contemplating a joint venture, you ought to be thinking about using it to bid contracts, not orders. If the purpose of the relationship is to go after orders, you're likely looking at a prime/subcontractor teaming relationship instead.

SIZES OF JOINT VENTURE PARTNERS

For all set-aside contracts (both small business set-asides and socioeconomic set-asides), each member of the joint venture ordinarily must qualify as a small business under the NAICS code assigned to the solicitation. If all members of the joint venture qualify as small, the joint venture does, too. But if any member of the joint venture exceeds the relevant size standard, the joint venture doesn't count as a small business and cannot be awarded the set-aside contract--except in the case of an SBA-approved mentor-protégé relationship.

EXAMPLE

MaryME IT and NowTech successfully perform work as a prime/subcontractor team. Now the two companies would like to pursue a stand-alone Navy solicitation, which has been issued as a small business set-aside. The solicitation is designated with NAICS code 541511 (Custom Computer Programming Services), with a corresponding $27.5 million size standard. MaryME's average annual receipts are $21 million; NowTech's are $9 million.

Result: Both companies are small businesses under the solicitation's size standard. If they wish, they may form a joint venture to pursue the work.

Wait a second. Don't SBA rules require us to add the sizes of joint venture partners together? If we do that here, MaryME and NowTech would have $30 million in collective receipts, exceeding the $27.5 million size standard.

The SBA's regulations did, in fact, used to specify that the sizes of joint venture partners would be added together in certain cases. But in 2016, the SBA changed the rules. Now, a joint venture qualifies for any set-aside contract so long as all of its members, individually, are "small" for that procurement. It makes no difference if the members' sizes, added together, exceed the size standard.

EXAMPLE

The Army issues a small business set-aside solicitation under NAICS code 621210 (Offices of Dentists), which carries an associated $7.5 million size standard. Duluth Tooth, Inc., a family dental practice located in Minnesota, has three-year average annual receipts of $2.0 million. Because the solicitation calls for services to be performed both in Minnesota and Wisconsin, Duluth Tooth wants to form a joint venture with Drill Sergeant Dentistry, a Milwaukee-based dental practice owned by a former Army Ranger.

Drill Sergeant's aggressive approach to good dental hygiene (such as requiring its patients to "drop and give me 50!" if they haven't flossed recently) has been very popular. As a result, Drill Sergeant's three-year average annual receipts are $10.0 million.

> **Result:** Because Drill Sergeant is a large business for purposes of the relevant NAICS code, a joint venture between Duluth Tooth and Drill Sergeant will not qualify as "small" for purposes of the Army solicitation—unless the companies take advantage of the mentor-protégé exception.

What should our mom-and-pop Minnesota dentists do now? Duluth Tooth can still team up with Drill Sergeant—just not as joint venture partners. Duluth Tooth and Drill Sergeant can execute a prime/subcontractor teaming agreement to pursue the work, and then a subcontract if Duluth Tooth wins the prime contract. There's nothing inherently wrong with a large business serving as a subcontractor on a set-aside contract.[11]

Our intrepid dental providers have another option: a powerful exception provided under one of the SBA's two mentor-protégé programs.

A federal mentor-protégé program is a vehicle under which a small business protégé receives various types of assistance from a mentor firm, which is usually larger and more experienced than the protégé (although a mentor need not necessarily be a *large* business so long as it has the experience, resources, and capabilities to assist the protégé). The mentor and protégé

---

[11] Of course, just because it's not inherently wrong doesn't mean that small businesses have unfettered discretion to work with large subcontractors. Set-aside contracts are subject to limitations on subcontracting, and the parties must also take care to avoid ostensible subcontractor affiliation.

negotiate and sign a written mentor-protégé agreement, which then must be approved by the sponsoring federal agency. Once the agency blesses the mentor-protégé agreement, the parties are entitled to certain benefits during the period the agreement is in effect.

Although many federal agencies sponsor mentor-protégé programs, we will focus exclusively on the two mentor-protégé programs run by the SBA: the 8(a) mentor-protégé program and the "All Small" mentor-protégé program. Importantly, *only* the SBA's mentor-protégé programs provide the special mentor-protégé joint venturing benefits we're about to discuss. Mentor-protégé programs run by other agencies (including the popular Department of Defense mentor-protégé program) don't confer any special joint venturing benefits—although these programs can offer other valuable perks.

MYTH VS REALITY

Myth: Participants in any federal mentor-protégé program may form joint ventures for set-aside contracts, and the size of the joint venture will be based solely on the protégé's size.

Reality: Only participants in the SBA's 8(a) and All Small mentor-protégé programs enjoy the special joint venture treatment. Participants in mentor-protégé programs operated by other federal agencies do not receive any special joint venturing benefits.

The SBA's 8(a) mentor-protégé program has been around for years, and has proven very popular. The problem was that participation as a protégé was limited to active 8(a) Program participants. Other small businesses wanted similar benefits, and began lobbying for a more inclusive SBA mentor-protégé program. In 2013, Congress authorized the SBA to create an expanded mentor-protégé program.

The SBA enacted its universal, or "All Small" mentor-protégé program in 2016. In the All Small mentor-protégé program, any business can participate as a protégé so long as it is small in its primary NAICS code, or in a secondary NAICS code in which it wishes to develop (and has already done some business). For more information on the All Small mentor-protégé program (and instructions on how to apply), visit the program's official website at https://www.sba.gov/navigation-structure/all-small-mentor-protege-program.

A joint venture comprised of an SBA-approved mentor and its protégé will count as "small" for any Federal prime contract or subcontract, provided that the protégé is a small business, and provided that the parties adopt a written joint venture agreement meeting certain requirements. In other words, when the members of a joint venture are an SBA-approved mentor and its protégé, and the joint venture agreement is structured properly, *the mentor's size doesn't count.*

> **EXAMPLE**
>
> Duluth Tooth's owners are impressed by Drill Sergeant's successful business, and want to learn the secrets of Drill Sergeant's success. Duluth Tooth and Drill Sergeant negotiate and execute a mentor-protégé agreement under the SBA's All Small mentor-protégé program, and the SBA approves the mentor-protégé agreement. The next month, the Air Force releases a solicitation under NAICS code 621210, with the associated $7.5 million size standard. Duluth Tooth and Drill Sergeant would like to form a joint venture to pursue the work. The companies' three-year average annual receipts are still $2.0 million and $10.0 million, respectively.
>
> **Result:** Because Duluth Tooth and Drill Sergeant are parties to an SBA-approved mentor-protégé agreement, they may joint venture for the Air Force solicitation without regard to Drill Sergeant's size. The companies may pursue the Air Force solicitation as joint venture partners.

For the special size rule to apply, the parties must have an *active* SBA mentor-protégé agreement in place as of the date the joint venture submits its initial proposal. If the agreement has yet to be approved or has expired (and all mentor-protégé agreements eventually expire), the mentor-protégé exception from affiliation won't apply.

Finally, it's important to be mindful of the fact that a mentor-protégé agreement is *not* a prerequisite to forming a joint venture unless one of the prospective joint venture partners is a large business. While mentor-protégé agreements can confer many useful benefits, their only relevance to joint ventures is to enable a large business to be part of a joint venture competing for a set-aside contract. Contrary to a common misconception, any small business (including an 8(a), SDVOSB, HUBZone, or WOSB) can joint venture with one or more other small businesses without a mentor-protégé agreement.

> **MYTH VS REALITY**
>
> **Myth:** To establish a joint venture for a federal contract, the prospective joint venture partners must first have an active SBA-approved mentor-protégé agreement.
>
> **Reality:** If both joint venture partners are small businesses under the size standard assigned to a set-aside solicitation, the companies can form a joint venture to compete on that solicitation without a mentor-protégé agreement.

Mentor-protégé agreements also don't exempt joint ventures from the mandatory rules on internal work share, profit splitting, subcontracting, and the like. We'll talk about these issues in Part IV.

SOCIOECONOMIC STATUS

Next up is the question of whether the joint venture qualifies for socioeconomic set-asides: contracts reserved exclusively for participants in the 8(a), SDVOSB/VOSB, HUBZone and WOSB/EDWOSB programs. In all four programs, a joint venture can qualify for award so long as one member (not all) holds the appropriate certification.

> **EXAMPLE**
> MaryME IT is a certified WOSB. NowTech is a certified HUBZone participant. The companies form a joint venture, MaryME Now, LLC, and properly structure it to comply with the WOSB joint venture rules. The joint venture submits a proposal for a NASA WOSB set-aside solicitation under NAICS code 541511.
> **Result:** Because MaryME IT is a WOSB, and because the joint venture was structured to satisfy the WOSB Program's rules, MaryME Now qualifies for award of the NASA solicitation.

NowTech isn't a WOSB, but it doesn't matter: the joint venture qualifies because MaryME IT has the correct socioeconomic certification, and the joint venture is structured appropriately.

> **EXAMPLE**
>
> After submitting a proposal to NASA, MaryME and NowTech come across a similar solicitation issued by the Department of Health and Human Services. The HHS solicitation is issued as a HUBZone set-aside. MaryME and NowTech want to use MaryME Now to submit a proposal.
>
> **Result:** MaryME Now is structured to bid on WOSB set-asides, not HUBZone set-asides. Even though one of its members is a HUBZone company, the joint venture doesn't qualify for the HHS solicitation.

As we'll discuss in detail in Part IV, a joint venture must be structured a certain way to qualify for a socioeconomic set-aside contract. For example, if an LLC like MaryME Now intends to bid on a WOSB set-aside, WOSBs must own at least 51% of the LLC, and a WOSB must serve as the joint venture's Managing Member. Similar rules apply for other socioeconomic categories.

Here, we know that MaryME Now qualifies for WOSB set-asides, which means that MaryME IT owns at least 51% of MaryME Now, and serves as the joint venture's Managing Member. Because NowTech, the HUBZone member, doesn't own the required percentage and doesn't serve as Managing Member, MaryME Now cannot qualify for HUBZone contracts.

Like MaryME IT and NowTech, small business owners often assume that a joint venture qualifies for award under any socioeconomic category that applies to either partner. Not so. Under the SBA's rules, a properly-constructed joint venture will take on the socioeconomic characteristics of its lead partner, but not those of other partners.

> **MYTH VS REALITY**
>
> **Myth:** A joint venture is eligible for socioeconomic contracts so long as any joint venture member has the appropriate certification.
>
> **Reality:** To qualify for a socioeconomic contract, the Managing Member must hold the appropriate certification. The joint venture doesn't qualify under socioeconomic certifications held only by other members.

That's not to say, of course, that MaryME IT and NowTech cannot pursue HUBZone set-aside contracts as joint venture partners. They can—but they need to establish a new HUBZone-compliant joint venture, one in which NowTech, the HUBZone firm, plays the lead role. If the parties establish a new joint venture (perhaps named "Now MaryME, LLC"), and the joint venture complies with the SBA's HUBZone regulations, that entity—though not MaryME Now—is eligible for HUBZone set-aside contracts.

THE "THREE-IN-TWO" RULE

We've probably given a couple dozen public presentations on joint venturing, and spoken about the topic one-on-one with hundreds of contractors. And in presentations and one-on-one conversations alike, perhaps the most common questions concern the SBA's so-called "three-in-two" rule. The three-in-two rule is:

- Very, very commonly misunderstood.
- At its core, little more than a "gotcha" for people who don't know about the three-in-two rule.
- Important to understand and comply with, so you're not on the wrong end of a "gotcha."

Before we delve into the specifics, it's helpful to understand why the three-in-two rule exists in the first place. From what we can tell, the rule stems from the SBA's view that a joint venture is a "limited-purpose business" that exists to carry on a handful of joint projects for a relatively brief period. A joint venture is not, in the SBA's eyes, a vehicle for "conducting business generally" on a "continuing or permanent basis."[12]

The three-in-two rule, then, exists to ensure that a joint venture is a limited-purpose entity. Under the rule, the parties to a joint venture may be deemed generally affiliated if the joint venture strays beyond the rule's established boundaries.

---

[12] 13 C.F.R. § 121.103(h).

> **MYTH VS REALITY**
>
> **Myth:** A joint venture cannot be awarded more than three contracts over a two-year period.
>
> **Reality:** The three-in-two rule does not limit the number of awards a joint venture can receive. Rather, it establishes that the joint venture members may become *generally affiliated* if a specific joint venture receives more than three contracts over a two-year period.

Most joint venturers, of course, don't want to be generally affiliated with their partners—which is why it's important to be mindful of the restrictions under the three-in-two rule. That said, there is a very common misunderstanding that the three-in-two rule prevents a joint venture from being awarded more than three contracts. Ordinarily, it doesn't. It's an affiliation rule, not a limit on contract awards.

The three-in-two rule says that the parties to a joint venture may be treated as affiliates when one of two circumstances exist:

1. More than two years after the joint venture was awarded its first contract, the joint venture submits a new proposal.
2. The joint venture has been awarded three or more contracts within the past two years, and submits a new proposal.

Let's look at an example of each component of the rule.

> **EXAMPLE**
>
> MaryME Now, the WOSB joint venture between MaryME IT and NowTech, is awarded its first contract on November 15, 2017. The joint venture submits several other bids but does not win any more work. On December 1, 2019, MaryME and NowTech spot a new WOSB solicitation and would like to submit a bid using MaryME Now.
>
> **Result:** More than two years have passed since MaryME Now was awarded its first contract. If MaryME Now submits a proposal, MaryME IT and NowTech may be deemed generally affiliated.

> **EXAMPLE**
>
> Duluth Tooth and Drill Sergeant form a joint venture named Tooth Drillers, LLC. The joint venture is awarded contracts on December 13, 2017, February 23, 2018, and May 19, 2018. On June 5, 2018, Tooth Drillers submits a proposal in response to a Coast Guard solicitation.
>
> **Result:** When it submitted its proposal, Tooth Drillers had been awarded three contracts within the past two years. The SBA may find Duluth Tooth and Drill Sergeant to be generally affiliated.

But what about the mentor-protégé agreement between Duluth Tooth and Drill Sergeant? Doesn't that shield the companies from affiliation?

Maybe. In a 2010 decision[13], the SBA Office of Hearings and Appeals suggested that the 8(a) mentor-protégé "shield" may protect a mentor and protégé from affiliation under the three-in-two rule. But as we'll discuss shortly, three-in-two violations are so easy to avoid that even SBA-approved mentor-protege pairs should take evasive action instead of relying on a potential exception from affiliation.

Before we get to evasive maneuvers, though, let's summarize the restrictions under the three-in-two rule. First, the rule says that a two-year clock starts ticking when a joint venture wins its first contract. Submit a proposal after that clock expires, and the joint venture partners could be affiliated. Second, the rule says that if the joint venture has been awarded three or more contracts within the past two years, it shouldn't submit any new proposals. Again, doing so may make the joint venture partners affiliated.

Importantly, the second piece of the rule applies to contracts awarded as of the date a new proposal is submitted—not contracts that eventually *could be* awarded.

EXAMPLE

Green Eggs 'n' Hamilton, the joint venture between Green Eggs, LLC and Hamilton Services, Inc., is awarded its first contract on November 21, 2017 and another contract on August 15, 2018. The joint venture submits an additional proposal on September 8, 2018 in response to a State Department solicitation. While the

---

[13] *Size Appeals of Safety and Ecology Corp.*, SBA No. SIZ-5177 (2010).

> State Department evaluation is ongoing, Green Eggs 'n' Hamilton submits a proposal in response to a NASA solicitation on September 30, 2018. On October 10, the State Department awards the contract to Green Eggs 'n' Hamilton.
>
> **Result:** As of September 30, Green Eggs 'n' Hamilton had not been awarded more than three contracts over the past two years. It did not violate the three-in-two rule by submitting a proposal, even though it ultimately was awarded the third contract.

Note that Green Eggs 'n' Hamilton could have had multiple proposals in the evaluation stage as of September 30, and eventually won them all, without violating the rule. So long as a joint venture has not been awarded more than three contracts over the past two years on the date the joint venture submits a bid, the joint venture won't violate the second piece of the three-in-two rule.

So that's the three-in-two rule. Now, let us reach for our soapbox so we can explain why we think the rule is a silly "gotcha." Actually, we'll just quote from the SBA regulation, which makes the point: "the same two (or more) entities may create additional joint ventures, and each new joint venture entity may be awarded up to three contracts in accordance with that section."

Yep, you read that right. The three-in-two rule is a limit on *joint venture entities*, not *joint venture partners*. When the parties reach one of the two regulatory limits, all they have to do is form a new joint venture, and the clock resets to zero.

Consider the real-life example of Dae Sung LLC and LB&B Associates, Inc., as reported in a SBA OHA case called *Size Appeal of Quality Services International, Inc.*, SBA No. SIZ-5599 (2014). Over a four-year period, Dae Sung and LB&B won 15 contracts as joint venture partners. But these companies were savvy, and spread those 15 contracts among eight separate joint venture entities. The result? No violation of the three-in-two rule. Had the venturers used a single joint venture entity, they likely would have been found affiliated.

What this means is that the same two companies can win the same contracts, worth the same amount, over the same period—and if they use the wrong number of joint ventures, they may be slapped with the harsh penalty of general affiliation; if they use the right number of joint ventures, there's no problem.

To us, this is craziness. The rule elevates form over substance. It makes a mockery of the SBA's affiliation rules, which say that the essence of any affiliation is "control." (How, exactly, is there any less control when the parties perform the same work with multiple joint ventures?) It forces small businesses to jump through unnecessary administrative and legal hoops and expend unnecessary resources, setting up new joint ventures with the same partners. And since it's so easy to circumvent the three-in-two rule, it is—in practice—little more than a "gotcha" for companies that don't know the three-in-two rule.

But (and please picture us saying this while climbing down from a soapbox), bad policy is still policy. The three-in-two rule is on the books, and SBA has given no signs that it's going anywhere. Know it, keep an eye on the two components, and form new joint ventures when needed.

One final note: taking "evasive action" to eliminate three-in-two problems doesn't mean that joint venture partners can *never* be found affiliated based on their relationship. Under the SBA's rules, "at some point . . . . such a longstanding inter-relationship or contractual dependence between the same joint venture partners will lead to a finding of general affiliation between and among them." When does a relationship between joint venture partners reach "some point"? The rules don't say.[14]

> **CHECK IT OUT: REGULATIONS DISCUSSED IN THIS PART**
> 13 C.F.R. § 121.103(h) (Joint Venture Size Rules & Three-in-Two Rule)
> FAR 9.6 (Contractor Team Arrangements)
> FAR 19.303 & 13 C.F.R. § 121.402 (Assignment of NAICS Codes)
> FAR 42.1204 (Novations)

---

[14] In the words of the U.S. Court of Federal Claims, "a regulation is unconstitutionally vague where it contains no standards by which the conduct it intends to prohibit can be ascertained." *Sutton v. United States*, 65 Fed.Cl. 800, 805 (2005). It will be interesting to see whether "at some point" passes the vagueness test if this language ever comes before a federal court (which, as of this writing, it apparently has not).

13 C.F.R. § 125.9 & 13 C.F.R. § 124.520 (SBA Mentor-Protégé Programs)

13 C.F.R. § 124.513 (8(a) Joint Ventures)

13 C.F.R. § 125.8 (Small Business Joint Ventures)

13 C.F.R. § 125.18 (SDVOSB & VOSB Joint Ventures)

13 C.F.R. § 126.616 (HUBZone Joint Ventures)

13 C.F.R. § 127.506 (WOSB & EDWOSB Joint Ventures)

PART III – JOINT VENTURE FORMATION

You're eligible to form a joint venture. And you're an adventurous soul, so what the heck—you're going to take the joint venture plunge!

Now what?

It's time for the nuts and bolts of forming a joint venture. And that means getting your hands dirty with some corporate paperwork. Let's get the fun started.

WRITING/OWN NAME

Under the SBA's regulations, a joint venture must "be in writing and must do business under its own name." The SBA does *not* require that a joint venture be a so-called "separate legal entity," that is, a legal entity formed with a state government, like a limited liability company or corporation. [15]

---

[15] As we'll discuss, though, even "informal" joint ventures are required to adopt written joint venture agreements.

Although the SBA doesn't specify what sort of "writing" must exist, a joint venture typically has a document called a *joint venture agreement*. As we'll see a little later in this chapter, joint venture agreements are required if the joint venture will pursue a socioeconomic set-aside and are also required if a mentor-protégé joint venture will pursue a small business set-aside.

While joint venture agreements are almost always used, many joint ventures also have other types of governing documents that supplement their joint venture agreements. For example, limited liability company joint ventures often adopt operating agreements, which contain additional corporate governance information outside the scope of a typical joint venture agreement.

In most cases, it's up to the parties to decide whether to adopt any sort of written agreement outside of a joint venture agreement (although, depending on the legal structure of the joint venture, some states' laws might require additional documentation). For joint ventures that do adopt additional corporate governance documentation, however, it is important to ensure that those additional documents do not conflict with or undermine any required provisions of the joint venture agreement.

EXAMPLE

Ate-Team LLC is an 8(a)-certified contractor providing catering services under primary NAICS code 722320 (Caterers). Ate-Team's unusual business approach includes writing "I pity the fool who doesn't contract with the Ate-Team!" on the cover of all its proposals. Ate-Team and a small business partner, Bee Team, Inc., form a LLC joint venture to pursue an Army 8(a) set-aside solicitation. As required by the SBA's 8(a) Program regulations, the parties' joint venture agreement calls for profits to be split according to each party's workshare. The two companies then execute an LLC operating agreement, which calls for profits to be split according to each party's ownership of the LLC.

Result: The profit-sharing provision of the operating agreement conflicts with the profit-sharing provision of the joint venture agreement. The SBA may decline to approve the joint venture for award of the 8(a) set-aside contract.

This isn't to say that LLC joint ventures shouldn't have operating agreements; they probably should in most cases. But the parties should carefully review each provision of the operating agreement to ensure that it is consistent with the joint venture agreement. It's also wise to insert a boilerplate provision in the operating agreement stating that, in the event of any conflict with the joint venture agreement, the joint venture agreement controls.

A compliant joint venture also must do business in its own name. If the joint venture has been formed with a state government, it should use the name the parties picked when the entity was formed. If not—if the joint venture is a less-formal partnership—the parties still must pick a name for their joint venture and use it when registering with SAM, preparing the proposal, and so on.

REGISTERED IN SAM

A joint venture must be registered in the System for Award Management (www.sam.gov) and identified as a joint venture in SAM. Of course, most companies who are thinking of forming joint ventures are already familiar with SAM and shouldn't have too much trouble registering the joint venture. For those that need some extra assistance, the local PTAC is often the best place to turn for free, hands-on assistance. Visit www.aptac-us.org to find the closest PTAC.

Of course, those familiar with SAM will say: "but I can't register in SAM without a DUNS number or CAGE code . . . and I can't get those without an EIN![16] Does my joint venture really need all these things?" Yep. Unless you or your PTAC counselor have come up with some special unique shortcut[17], there's no

---

[16] For the uninitiated, an EIN is an Employer Identification Number, which is obtained through the IRS. A DUNS number is a unique nine-digit identification number assigned by Dun & Bradstreet, and is required for federal contractors. A CAGE code is a separate five-digit identification number assigned by the Defense Logistics Agency. Talk to your PTAC counselor if you need help obtaining these numbers.

[17] If you have, please share it with the contracting community. A guest blog on *SmallGovCon* would be a great place to start. You'll be a hero to a lot of frustrated SAM users.

other way to get on SAM except by also obtaining an EIN, DUNS, and CAGE code. Sorry.

UNPOPULATED SEPARATE LEGAL ENTITY

As noted above, a joint venture can take various legal structures. Perhaps most common is the LLC, which in many states offers an appealing combination of favorable tax treatment, flexible rules involving internal governance, and (as the name suggests) limitations on the liability of the LLC members for the LLC's liabilities. An entity like an LLC or corporation must be formed by filing paperwork with a state government and receiving confirmation from the state government that the entity exists. The SBA uses the term "separate legal entity" to describe joint ventures that are formed by filing paperwork with a state government.

A joint venture can also take the form of a partnership, which often is not formed with a state government. The partners sign their joint venture agreement, and that act alone creates the partnership. When a joint venture is created without filing paperwork with a state government, the SBA views this arrangement as "informal" and *not* creating a "separate legal entity." That terminology, while legally accurate, is somewhat misleading: a partnership still is an "entity," it's just not considered "separate" from its partners for liability purposes—that is, the partners are fully liable for the debts of the partnership.

Our quibbles with the confusing terminology aside, this discussion is important because the SBA's regulations state that a separate legal entity joint venture, such as an LLC, must be *unpopulated*. An unpopulated joint venture is one that does not have its own employees to perform the work required under a government contract. The SBA's restriction is relatively new; before mid-2016, the SBA allowed all joint ventures to be either populated or unpopulated.

> **EXAMPLE**
>
> Ate-Team LLC and Bee Team Inc. have formed a joint venture using the LLC legal structure, and have named their creation Ate-Bee JV LLC. Bee Team Inc. is concerned that Ate-Team's employees aren't up to the task of handling a large share of the catering duties called for in a new Navy set-aside solicitation. The parties decide that Ate-Bee JV LLC will hire its own employees to perform the Navy contract—and 95% of them will come from Bee Team.
>
> **Result:** Ate-Bee JV LLC is a populated entity and thus does not qualify as a joint venture.

The restriction on populated joint ventures exists only with respect to individuals who will perform the contract's scope of work. If the parties wish, they can hire one or more administrative personnel (such as a bookkeeper) to work directly for the joint venture.[18] Most joint venturers, however, don't put anyone—administrative personnel or otherwise—on the payroll of an unpopulated joint venture.

Finally, it's an open question as to whether the SBA intended to allow informal joint ventures—again, those that aren't organized with a state government—to be populated. We don't see a reason why such entities would be allowed to have employees, while LLCs and other separate legal entities would not. And in conversations with some SBA officials, we get the sense that the SBA intended to prohibit any joint venture (formal or informal) from being populated. That said, the issue has yet to be definitively resolved.

MANDATORY JOINT VENTURE PROVISIONS

When a joint venture between two or more small businesses will pursue a small business set-aside contract, the parties must adopt a written joint venture agreement, but there are no legal requirements for what the joint venture agreement must contain. But for many set-aside contracts, a joint venture agreement must contain certain mandatory provisions. If the agreement omits

---

[18] Because the Defense Security Service won't grant a facility security clearance to an entity it views as unpopulated, some joint venturers have added a Facility Security Officer to a joint venture's payroll in an effort to obtain an FCL. In theory, anyway, this arrangement makes the joint venture "populated" for DSS purposes, but "unpopuluated" for SBA purposes. Unfortunately, however, the interplay between the SBA's joint venture rules and the government's security clearance requirements is an evolving area of law, with little definitive guidance.

even one of these provisions (or contains language restricting or undercutting those mandatory provisions), the agreement is invalid.

The specific required provisions vary slightly depending on the contract the joint venture will pursue:

- If a mentor-protégé joint venture will pursue a small business set-aside contract, the joint venture agreement must comply with the requirements of 13 C.F.R. § 125.8(b). Additionally, due to a quirk in the regulations, a joint venture established under the 8(a) mentor-protégé program may *also* need to comply with the separate requirements under 13 C.F.R. § 124.513(c) in order for the joint venture to avail itself of the mentor-protégé exception from affiliation. Fortunately, after some SBA regulatory clean-up in late 2016, the regulations no longer conflict with one another.
- If the joint venture will pursue an 8(a) set-aside or sole source contract, the joint venture agreement must comply with the requirements of 13 C.F.R. § 124.513(c).
- If the joint venture will pursue an SDVOSB or VOSB set-aside contract or sole source contract, the joint venture agreement must comply with the requirements of 13 C.F.R. § 125.18(b)(2). This requirement applies even if the procuring agency is the U.S. Department of Veterans Affairs; the VA defers to the SBA's rules governing SDVOSB joint venture agreements.

- If the joint venture will pursue a HUBZone set-aside or sole source contract, the joint venture agreement must comply with the requirements of 13 CF.R. § 126.616(c).
- If the joint venture will pursue a WOSB or EDWOSB set-aside or sole source contract, the joint venture agreement must comply with the requirements of 13 C.F.R. § 127.506(c).

Fortunately, the requirements of the five separate regulations are very similar (although not completely identical). A consolidated description of those requirements—as of the date of this Handbook—is next.

But first, a note of caution: *the discussion below is not a substitute for reading and complying with the regulations*. In recent years, the SBA has tinkered quite a bit with the joint venture requirements—what you read below may not be complete or up-to-date. Anyone forming a joint venture must independently ensure that the joint venture agreement meets the precise, current requirements of the appropriate regulatory provision.[19]

---

[19] For further reading, please see the giant disclaimer on the first page of this book.

A WORD ABOUT JOINT VENTURE AGREEMENT "TEMPLATES"

A joint venture agreement *must* include every mandatory legal requirement. Missing even one mandatory requirement can lead to the joint venture being declared ineligible. But despite the crucial importance of getting the joint venture agreement exactly right, many small businesses attempt to cut costs by using "templates" from various sources, including questionable Internet domains. While the right template can make a good starting point, it is no substitute for ensuring that the joint venture agreement fully complies with the appropriate regulatory requirements. Following the SBA's major overhaul of its joint venture regulations in 2016, many templates are outdated.[20] And even those that are not outdated haven't necessarily been vetted for legal compliance. Buyer (or downloader) beware.

The consolidated description of the mandatory joint venture agreement requirements under the five regulations is as follows:[21]

---

[20] Unfortunately, this includes templates offered by some SBA District Offices themselves, primarily to 8(a) participants. In the months following the SBA's 2016 regulatory changes, some District Offices continued sending outdated templates to small businesses that asked for help. Hopefully, these problems will soon be resolved, but the unfortunate truth is that not even a template from the SBA is guaranteed to be correct.

[21] This discussion assumes that the joint venture will be comprised of only two companies, which is by far the most common joint venture arrangement. A few of the requirements will vary if the joint venture is comprised of more than two companies.

1. *Purpose.* A joint venture agreement must contain a provision setting forth the purpose of the joint venture. Ordinarily, the stated purpose is to pursue a specific solicitation, or to pursue multiple solicitations. This is an easy requirement to meet; the only way to get it "wrong" is to omit it.

2. *Managing Venturer.* A qualified business (by size and socioeconomic criteria) must be named the Managing Venturer of the joint venture. So, for example, if the joint venture will pursue an SDVOSB set-aside contract, an eligible SDVOSB must be named Managing Venturer.

    Although this one sounds simple, it's an easy one to undermine if the parties insert provisions that make it clear that the Managing Venturer doesn't enjoy the power to, you know, *manage*. We'll talk about this more in the next section, which is conveniently named "Don't Undermine Mandatory Joint Venture Provisions."

3. *Project Manager.* An employee of the Managing Venturer must be named the Project Manager responsible for performance of the contract. Although the regulations are not crystal clear on this point, the SBA's administrative judges have held that this requirement necessitates naming an actual person, not just vaguely stating that "an employee" of the Managing Venturer will serve in that role.

Under four of the five regulations, the Project Manager can be a contingent hire—that is, someone who is not on the Managing Venturer's staff at the time the proposal is submitted, but has agreed to join the Managing Venturer if the joint venture wins the contract. Contingent hires are, of course, very common in government contracting: small businesses don't always have highly-compensated individuals like Project Managers sitting around the office playing Minesweeper and waiting for a potential contract award. If the Project Manager will be a contingent hire, he or she must sign a letter of intent committing to be employed by the Managing Venturer if the joint venture wins the contract.

While contingent hires are generally permitted, if the joint venture consists of a mentor and its protégé, the Project Manager cannot be employed by the mentor and become an employee of the protégé for purposes of the set-aside or sole source contract. SBA, apparently, thinks that such an arrangement confers too much power on the mentor.

What if the partner venturer is not a mentor—can the Project Manager be a contingent hire from the partner? The SBA's regulations use the word "mentor" to describe the restriction, which shouldn't apply to a non-mentor partner. But the regulation is new, and as of this writing, there's no case law interpreting whether SBA intended the restriction to be broader. Tread carefully.

Oddly, no provision for contingent hires is included in the regulations governing SDVOSB contracts. While this may be a regulatory oversight on the SBA's part, it would be wise for joint ventures pursuing SDVOSB contracts to assume that the regulation requires that the Project Manager be employed by the Managing Venturer as of the date the joint venture submits its proposal. (But check back on this one: if it's a regulatory oversight, the SBA may have amended its regulations by the time you read this).

4. *Profits.* The Managing Venturer (and any other joint venture partners holding the appropriate size/socioeconomic designation) must receive profits commensurate with their work share. As we'll discuss below, the SBA requires that the Managing Venturer (again, combined with any other joint venture partners holding the appropriate size/socioeconomic designation) perform at least 40% of the joint venture's work. Therefore, the Managing Venturer[22] must receive at least 40% of the joint venture's profits.

---

[22] Almost all government contracts joint ventures consist of just two parties, although it's allowable to have multi-party JVs. To make this chapter easier to read (and easier for us to write), we're going to stop saying "in conjunction with any other joint venture partners holding the appropriate size/socioeconomic designation." That said, if you're planning a multi-member JV, check the regulations very carefully to see which functions can be divvied up among multiple qualifying members, and which cannot.

The profit-splitting provisions underwent multiple revisions between 2011 and 2016 and are a continuing source of confusion. You may run across joint venture templates that require profits to be split commensurate with equity ownership; those templates are outdated. You may also see joint venture templates that call for different formulas depending on whether the joint venture is populated or unpopulated. Those, too, are outdated (as is the concept of populated JV itself).

The regulations don't discuss *when* profits must be divided—that's up to the parties to decide. The regulations also don't discuss how the parties must apportion losses. That said, it's typical for the parties to agree to apportion losses in the same manner as profits.

5. *Ownership.* Under all five regulations, if the joint venture is a separate legal entity (almost always, a limited liability company), the joint venture agreement must specify that the Managing Member owns at least 51% of the joint venture. A 51/49 ownership split is the norm, although the Managing Member can own more than 51%.

6. *Special Bank Account.* Under all five regulations, the joint venture agreement must provide for the establishment and administration of a so-called "special bank account," which is just an operating account. The account must require the signature of both parties (or their designees) for

withdrawal purposes.[23] All payments due the joint venture for the set-aside contract must be deposited in the special bank account; all expenses incurred under the set-aside contract must be paid from the account, as well.

7. *Equipment, Facilities and Resources.* The joint venture agreement ordinarily must itemize all major facilities, equipment, and resources to be furnished by each party. Additionally, "where practical," the parties must provide a detailed schedule of the cost or value of the listed facilities, equipment and resources. It's not entirely clear when the SBA will deem it impractical to provide the list; when in doubt, the list is a very good idea.

The SBA does provide an exception where the contract is "indefinite in nature," such as an indefinite delivery/indefinite quantity (IDIQ) contract. In such a case, the joint venture agreement may either: (a) provide a general description of the anticipated major facilities, equipment and resources to be furnished by each party, without a detailed schedule of cost or value of each; or (b) specify how the parties will furnish such resources to the joint venture once a definite scope of work is made publicly available.

---

[23] This requirement was originally written in an era of paper checks and deposit slips. Many of our clients question whether it still makes sense in the age of electronic banking; even the Government pays contractors electronically much of the time. We think it would be a good idea for the SBA to revisit this rule, but for now, it's still on the books as-is.

Note that this exception applies to indefinite contracts only. When the solicitation includes a definite scope of work, the parties must itemize major equipment, facilities, and resources.

8. *Negotiation of the Contract.* The joint venture agreement must specify the responsibilities of the parties with respect to negotiation of the prime contract with the government. Typically, the parties specify that the Managing Venturer (represented by the Project Manager or a corporate officer) will play the lead role. While there's nothing directly prohibiting the partner venturer from playing the lead role in negotiations, such an arrangement may cause the SBA to question whether the Managing Venturer really has managerial authority.

9. *Source of Labor.* The joint venture agreement must specify each party's role with respect to the sources of labor to be used for the contract. This requirement can be very specific to the set-aside solicitation in question, but the parties often specify that, for example, certain existing employees will perform work, that the joint venture will attempt to hire incumbent employees for certain positions, and so on.

For an IDIQ or other contract where the level of effort or scope of work is not known, the joint venture agreement must either: (a) provide a general description of the parties' anticipated responsibilities with respect to the source of labor; or (b) specify how the parties will define such responsibilities once a definitive scope of work is made publicly available.

10. *Contract Performance.* The joint venture agreement must specify the responsibilities of the parties with respect to contract performance. Some detail is required here: the equivalent of "we'll figure it out later" usually isn't good enough. There is an exception, though, for IDIQ and other indefinite contracts. As with negotiation and source of labor, the joint venture agreement may either: (a) provide a general description of the anticipated responsibilities of the parties with regard to contract performance; or (b) specify how the parties will define such responsibilities once a definitive scope of work is made publicly available.

11. *Performance of Work.* The joint venture agreement must set forth how the parties will ensure compliance with the applicable performance of work requirements. We will discuss the performance of work requirements themselves (with several examples) in the next chapter.

    Note that the parties must specify *how* they intend to ensure compliance with these requirements. For example, the joint venture agreement might state that the Project Manager will monitor compliance and report monthly to the Managing Venturer, which will adjust work assignments if needed to ensure ongoing compliance.

Merely parroting the requirements themselves isn't good enough—that doesn't answer the "how" question.

12. *Ensured Performance.* The joint venture agreement must contain a provision obligating all parties to the joint venture to ensure performance of the set-aside contract and to complete performance despite the withdrawal of any other member.

13. *Accounting and Administrative Records.* The joint venture agreement must contain a provision stating that accounting and other administrative records are to be kept in the office of the Managing Venturer, unless the SBA grants written approval to keep them elsewhere.

    This regulation, which was originally drafted in a world where "records" meant "paper" probably should be updated to reflect the fact that modern joint venturers often keep many of their records on cloud-based systems, readily accessible in real-time to both parties. We have yet to see the SBA have a problem with a cloud-based arrangement, but we suppose there's a first time for everything.

14. *Final Original Records.* The joint venture agreement must contain a provision requiring the final original records be retained by the Managing Venturer. Often, the parties specify that the partner venturer will keep a copy of the records, but this isn't required.

15. *Quarterly Financial Statements.* The joint venture agreement must contain a provision stating that "quarterly financial statements showing cumulative contract receipts and expenditures (including salaries of the joint venture's principals) must be submitted to SBA not later than 45 days after each operating quarter of the joint venture."

16. *Profit-and-Loss Statement.* The joint venture agreement must contain a statement that "a project-end profit and loss statement, including a statement of final profit distribution, must be submitted to the SBA no later than 90 days after completion of the contract."[24]

There—that was simple enough, right? A mere 16 required provisions, and no margin for error if you get any of them wrong.

Again, check (and double check) any joint venture agreement against the required regulations before signing it, and don't use this Handbook as gospel—only the current version of the appropriate regulation can tell you whether you're in compliance.

DON'T UNDERMINE MANDATORY JOINT VENTURE PROVISIONS

Sometimes, joint venturers get the required provisions right, but then adopt additional provisions undercutting those

---

[24] Yes, in all five regulations, the SBA uses the phrase "*not* later than 45 days" but then uses "*no* later than 90 days." Are we the only ones who've noticed this odd difference? Does this mean we spend too much time looking at SBA regulations? Never mind, don't answer that.

requirements. These additional provisions sometimes are inserted in the joint venture agreement itself, but often they're in a separate agreement, such as an LLC's operating agreement. Additional provisions that undercut any of the 16 requirements can cause the joint venture to be noncompliant, and ineligible for award of a set-aside contract.

> **EXAMPLE**
>
> Duluth Tooth is owned and controlled by a woman, Lucy Demuth. Duluth Tooth becomes certified in the woman-owned small business program. After receiving its WOSB certification, Duluth Tooth spots a WOSB set-aside solicitation for dental services. Duluth Tooth and Drill Sergeant Dentistry begin negotiating a new joint venture agreement to pursue the solicitation. The joint venture agreement includes all the provisions required by the WOSB program regulations. Drill Sergeant's lawyers then mark up the agreement to add a requirement that the joint venture establish a Board of Managers, comprised of two representatives from each party, and that for all "tactical and business" decisions of the Company, the votes of two-thirds of the Board members are required.
>
> **Result**: The two-thirds voting requirement means that Duluth Tooth cannot make tactical or business decisions for the joint venture without Drill Sergeants' approval. This provision undercuts the requirement that Duluth Tooth, the WOSB, serve

> as Managing Venturer, and likely renders the joint venture ineligible for the WOSB set-aside contract.

While Lucy and her company are figments of our imagination, this situation isn't. In fact, it's based on a real SBA OHA decision in which this exact requirement caused a joint venture to be ineligible for a SDVOSB set-aside contract.[25]

A small or socioeconomically disadvantaged business negotiating with a larger partner must be especially vigilant, as some larger partners are prone to proposing provisions that undercut the small Managing Venturer's role as manager. We've seen, for example, agreements in which the partner proposed its own coequal Project Manager (non-compliant) or proposed sweeping unanimity provisions like the sort suggested by Drill Sergeant's lawyers. Remember, while large partners understandably want the biggest piece of pie they can get, a non-compliant joint venture agreement hurts everyone—no one wins if the joint venture is successfully protested, or disapproved by the SBA. Negotiate accordingly.

AMENDING JOINT VENTURES

As you undoubtedly noticed, some of the mandatory joint venture provisions are contract-specific; that is, they are very

---

[25] *See SOF Associates-JV*, SBA No. VET-234 (2013).

likely to change depending on the solicitation the joint venture is bidding. Things like the identity of the Project Manager and the division of work aren't going to stay the same from one solicitation to another.

Does that mean that a new joint venture agreement is required each time the parties pursue a contract? Fortunately, the answer is "no."

Instead of preparing an entirely new joint venture agreement each time the joint venture goes after a different solicitation, the parties often can simply sign a short amendment or addendum to the initial joint venture agreement. The amendment or addendum changes the project-specific items, but keeps everything else (the bulk of the joint venture agreement) in place. This can save a lot of time and effort.

In fact, forward-thinking partners can put together what we call a "generic" initial joint venture agreement—that is, one that doesn't contain any of the project-specific items. A generic joint venture can be useful when the parties anticipate pursuing solicitations that might be issued with a relatively short response time and want to get their documents squared away in advance. That way, when a solicitation is issued, all the parties must do is execute a short amendment or addendum, and they're good to go.

In its 2016 regulatory changes, the SBA endorsed the concept, although the SBA didn't use the word "generic." The SBA's 8(a) regulations now state that an 8(a) participant "may submit a joint venture agreement to SBA for approval at any time, whether or not in connection with a specific 8(a) procurement."

When using a generic joint venture agreement, be careful: the project-specific amendment or addendum must be executed before the initial proposal is submitted. If the parties forget to do so, the joint venture agreement is incomplete, and the joint venture could be ineligible for award.

Finally, don't forget about the three-in-two rule we discussed in the last chapter. Joint venture amendments and addenda are very useful, and it saves time and effort to use them when appropriate. But when one of the three-in-two thresholds is met, it's time to play the SBA's game and form a new joint venture.

PRIOR APPROVAL OF JOINT VENTURES

For a joint venture to be awarded an 8(a) contract, the SBA must approve the joint venture prior to award of the contract. Additionally, for a joint venture to be awarded a VA SDVOSB or VOSB contract, the joint venture must be separately verified by the VA Center for Verification and Evaluation prior to submission of its proposal. (There is no requirement that the VA verify a joint venture before it bids on a *non-VA* SDVOSB solicitation).

That's it. Despite a very common misconception, joint ventures for other types of contracts *do not* require prior approval by the SBA or anyone else (although a mentor-protégé joint venture must have an SBA-approved mentor-protégé agreement in place to avail itself of the special exception from affiliation).

> **MYTH VS REALITY**
>
> **Myth:** The SBA must grant prior approval for all joint ventures bidding on all types of set-aside contracts.
>
> **Reality:** The SBA's prior approval is only required for 8(a) contracts.

> **EXAMPLE**
>
> Ate-Team, LLC (an 8(a) Program participant) and Bee Team, Inc. (a small business) form a new joint venture to pursue a NASA small business set-aside contract. The joint venturers do not seek the SBA's prior approval of its joint venture agreement.
>
> **Result:** The SBA's prior approval is not necessary for a joint venture to pursue a small business set-aside contract—even where, as here, one of the joint venturers is an 8(a) Program participant.

The SBA's prior approval is not necessary for a joint venture to be awarded small business, HUBZone, WOSB, or SDVOSB contracts. And as the example demonstrates, it is the set-aside designation for the solicitation—not the Managing Member's socioeconomic status—that determines whether the prior approval of the SBA or VA is required.

The SBA approves 8(a) joint ventures on a contract-by-contract basis. If a joint venture has been approved for one 8(a) contract, it is not automatically eligible for another 8(a) contract. Instead, the joint venturers must execute an amendment or addendum to the joint venture agreement, changing those pieces of the original joint venture agreement that are contract-specific—such as the identity of the project manager, the anticipated work split between the parties, and each party's role in providing labor, equipment, facilities and resources to the joint venture. The SBA must separately approve the amendment or addendum before the joint venture can be awarded a new 8(a) contract.

> **MYTH VS REALITY**
>
> **Myth:** Once a joint venture has been approved by the SBA for one 8(a) contract, the joint venture is "8(a) certified" and can pursue additional 8(a) contracts without SBA permission.
>
> **Reality:** The SBA's approval is required each time a joint venture pursues an 8(a) contract. If the joint venture has already been approved for one 8(a) contract, the SBA must approve an amendment or addendum to the original joint venture agreement in order for the joint venture to pursue a second 8(a) contract.

The VA must verify a joint venture before the joint venture can validly *submit a proposal* for a VA SDVOSB or VOSB set-aside contract. This is, of course, different than the SBA's 8(a) requirement, which merely requires approval before award.

The VA's policy can make a joint venture a risky idea when a relatively short time remains before proposals are due. The VA's processing time for joint ventures varies, but it's wise to assume that it could take as much as two to three months (although it could be considerably shorter). If there's a risk that the joint venture won't be verified by the bid date, the parties should be prepared with a backup plan: bidding a prime/subcontractor team.

Although the VA insists on verification before the proposal date, the VA does not require that the joint venture be verified again each time it pursues a contract. Once the joint venture is verified, the parties can amend the joint venture agreement to pursue additional solicitations.

CHECK IT OUT: REGULATIONS DISCUSSED IN THIS PART

13 C.F.R. § 121.103(h) (Joint Venture Size Rules & Three-in-Two Rule)

13 C.F.R. § 125.9 & 13 C.F.R. § 124.520 (SBA Mentor-Protégé Programs)

13 C.F.R. § 124.513 (8(a) Joint Ventures)

13 C.F.R. § 125.8 (Small Business Joint Ventures)

13 C.F.R. § 125.18 (SDVOSB & VOSB Joint Ventures)

13 C.F.R. § 126.616 (HUBZone Joint Ventures)

13 C.F.R. § 127.506 (WOSB & EDWOSB Joint Ventures)

48 C.F.R. § 819.7003; 48 C.F.R. § 852.219-10; & 48 C.F.R. § 852.219-11 (VA SDVOSB & VOSB Joint Ventures)

PART IV – JOINT VENTURE PERFORMANCE

Congratulations! Your joint venture has won a federal prime contract. Now it's time to successfully perform the contract—and split the profits.

This chapter is all about the special rules governing performance of a contract by a joint venture. We'll start with the two performance of work requirements: first, how much the joint venture can subcontract to third parties, and second, how the joint venture must allocate the remaining work among its members. The interplay between these two requirements tends to twist contractors' brains into knots, so we'll walk through a few examples for clarity.

We'll finish Part IV (and this Handbook) by talking about required certificates of compliance, performance of work reports, and the SBA's right to inspect the joint venture's records.

PERFORMANCE OF WORK REQUIREMENTS

A joint venture performing work on a set-aside contract must comply with two equally important work share requirements (also known as "performance of work" requirements).

First, the joint venture—as prime contract(ors)—must comply with the applicable limitation on subcontracting. This first requirement compares the work performed by the joint venture, on the one hand, to the work performed by the joint venture's subcontractors, on the other.

> **EXAMPLE**
>
> Learning from their prior mistakes, Duluth Tooth and Drill Sergeant revise their joint venture agreement to comply with the WOSB program regulations. The joint venture bids on a WOSB set-aside contract under NAICS code 621210 (Offices of Dentists). Lucy, eager to comply with all applicable regulations, tells Drill Sergeant that the SBA regulations require Duluth Tooth to receive at least 50% of the amount paid by the government under the WOSB contract.
>
> **Result:** Lucy's intentions are admirable, but she's mistaken. The joint venture—not Duluth Tooth—is the WOSB prime contractor. The FAR and SBA regulations require the joint venture as a whole—not Duluth Tooth individually—to subcontract no more than 50% of the amount paid by the government (excepting subcontracts to similarly situated entities).

> **MYTH VS REALITY**
>
> **Myth:** When a joint venture wins a set-aside contract, the limitations on subcontracting apply to the Managing Member of the joint venture.
>
> **Reality:** A joint venture is the prime contractor. The limitations on subcontracting apply to the joint venture *as a whole*, not the Managing Member individually.

In our experience, it is very common for contractors to become confused about how the limitations on subcontracting apply to joint ventures. Remember: the limitations on subcontracting have nothing to do with the work split between the members of a joint venture. They apply only to the division of work between the joint venture and its subcontractors (if any).

We will cover the limitations on subcontracting in detail in a future Handbook in this series—so keep your eyes peeled. In the meantime, you should review the SBA's regulations at 13 C.F.R. § 125.6.[26]

---

[26] As of the publication of this Handbook, the FAR Council had yet to update the FAR to conform with the SBA's regulation and the underlying statute, which was amended by the 2013 National Defense Authorization Act. Hopefully, this confusion will soon be resolved.

JOINT VENTURE INTERNAL WORK SHARE REQUIREMENTS

Just because a joint venture, collectively, serves as the prime contractor doesn't mean that the joint venture partners are free to split the work any way they want. That's true for some joint ventures: when two or more small businesses form a joint venture to bid on a small business set-aside contract, there are no internal work split requirements. Ditto for joint ventures pursuing unrestricted procurements. But when a joint venture will pursue an 8(a), SDVOSB, HUBZone or WOSB contract, or when a mentor-protégé joint venture will pursue a small business set-aside contract, the Managing Venturer—either alone or in conjunction with other eligible joint venture partners—must perform at least 40% of the work to be performed by the joint venture.

EXAMPLE

MaryME IT, LLC forms a joint venture with NowTech, Inc. The joint venture, MaryME Now LLC, will bid on a NASA small business set-aside solicitation under NAICS code 541430 (Graphic Design Services) with a corresponding $7.5 million size standard. MaryME IT and NowTech are both small businesses under the solicitation's size standard. In negotiations between the parties, Mary insists on performing 75% of the joint venture's work.

Result: Because both joint venturers are small businesses, they may split the work any way they wish. If Mary can convince NowTech to agree to her proposal, MaryME IT can perform 75% of the joint venture's work.

EXAMPLE

Duluth Tooth Inc. and Drill Sergeant Dentistry are parties to an SBA-approved 8(a) mentor-protégé agreement. They form a new joint venture, Duluth Tooth Twoth, to bid on a Navy 8(a) set-aside contract under NAICS code 621210 (Offices of Dentists), which carries an associated $7.5 million size standard. Duluth Tooth is an 8(a) participant and small business under NAICS code 621210; Drill Sergeant is neither 8(a)-certified nor small (although it is Duluth Tooth's SBA-approved mentor). In negotiations, Drill Sergeant's owner, Henry "Sarge" Kelley, insists that his company perform 75% of the joint venture's work.

Result: Drill Sergeant's size is disregarded because of the mentor-protégé agreement. However, because the solicitation is for an 8(a) contract, 8(a) small businesses must perform at least 40% of the joint venture's work. Sarge's proposed arrangement is non-compliant.

> **MYTH VS REALITY**
>
> **Myth:** A mentor-protégé joint venture has no internal work share requirements; the mentor can perform all or almost all of the joint venture's work.
>
> **Reality:** A mentor-protégé joint venture is subject to the same internal work share requirements as any other joint venture. If the joint venture is awarded a set-aside contract, the mentor can perform no more than 60% of the joint venture's work.

Keep in mind that the 40% number applies to the joint venture's portion of the overall work, not the entire value of the contract. If the joint venture has subcontractors, the work performed by those subcontractors is disregarded in calculating compliance with the 40% requirement—unless the subcontractor is one of the members.

> **EXAMPLE**
>
> After Sarge reconsiders his aggressive work share demand, Duluth Tooth Twoth wins the Navy 8(a) set-aside contract. The total value of the contract is $10 million. The joint venture decides to subcontract half of the work, $5 million, to a non-8(a) subcontractor. Duluth Tooth and Drill Sergeants will split the remainder of the work equally, with each receiving $2.5 million.
>
> **Result:** Duluth Tooth will perform 50% of the joint venture's work ($2.5 million out of $5 million). Since Duluth Tooth will

> perform more than 40% of the joint venture's work, the arrangement is compliant.

In this case, Duluth Tooth—the 8(a) Managing Venturer—will ultimately receive only 25% of the total paid under the contract. But because the amount subcontracted isn't considered in the internal work share analysis, Duluth Tooth Twoth remains on the right side of the law.

In determining whether the Managing Venturer will perform at least 40% of the work, the SBA will aggregate the work performed by the other party at all tiers. In other words, a non-Managing Venturer cannot circumvent the 40% rule by becoming a subcontractor to the joint venture.

EXAMPLE
Fresh off its success with the Navy 8(a) set-aside, Duluth Tooth Twoth pursues and wins a similar contract for the Marine Corps. Like the Navy contract, the USMC contract has a total value of $10 million and is an 8(a) set-aside. Sarge proposes that the joint venture split the work the same way it did last time: $2.5 million for Duluth Tooth and $2.5 million for Drill Sergeants. Sarge suggests that the joint venture subcontract the remaining $5 million to Drill Sergeants.
Result: The SBA will aggregate the work performed by Drill Sergeants at both tiers. After the aggregation, Drill Sergeants is performing $7.5 million (75%) and Duluth Tooth $2.5 million

> (25%). The arrangement doesn't comply with the 40% minimum requirement for Duluth Tooth.

The aggregation rule applies to affiliates of the non-Managing Venturer, too. For example, let's say that Sarge owns a second dental practice, named Drill Baby Drill, Inc. A subcontract to Drill Baby Drill—an affiliate of Drill Sergeants—would be treated no differently than a subcontract to Drill Sergeants itself.

TYPE OF WORK PERFORMED

In addition to the 40% requirement, the Managing Venturer (alone or in conjunction with other companies holding the appropriate socioeconomic classification) must perform work that is "more than administrative or ministerial functions so that they gain substantive experience." However, the SBA's regulations don't provide any guidance as to when a company's work crosses the line into mere "administrative or ministerial functions." Contractors will have to use a dose of common sense.

CERTIFICATIONS AND REPORTS

If a joint venture submits a proposal for a socioeconomic set-aside contract (8(a), SDVOSB, HUBZone, or WOSB), or if a mentor-protégé joint venture submits a proposal for a small business set-aside contract, the Managing Member of the joint venture must submit a written certification to the SBA and agency Contracting Officer prior to the performance of the contract. The certification must be signed by an authorized official of each partner to the joint venture, and must state as follows:

- The parties have entered into a joint venture agreement that fully complies with the applicable regulations. Here, the parties should specifically cite the regulation that they have followed (e.g., 13 C.F.R. § 125.18(b)(2) for an SDVOSB joint venture).
- The parties will perform the contract in compliance with the joint venture agreement and the performance of work requirements set forth in the applicable regulation. Again, the parties should specifically cite to the correct regulation (e.g., 13 C.F.R. § 124.513(c) for an 8(a) joint venture).

For 8(a) joint ventures only, the certification must also state that the parties have obtained the SBA's approval of the joint venture agreement and any addendum to that agreement and that there have been no modifications to the agreement that the SBA has not approved.

For WOSB contracts only, the WOSB Managing Venturer must provide a copy of the joint venture agreement to the agency Contracting Officer. Of course, for other contracts, Contracting Officers retain the discretion to require such documentation as well—and some do, to better assure themselves that the joint venture is eligible.

In addition to the certifications required on the front end, for the four categories of socioeconomic set-asides, as well as mentor-protégé joint ventures performing small business set-asides, the Managing Venturer must provide the following reports:

- An annual report to the Contracting Officer and the SBA, signed by an authorized official of each joint venturer, explaining how the performance of work requirements are being met for the contract. Although not specified in the regulation, the intent appears to be that the report address compliance both with the applicable limitation on subcontracting and with the internal work share requirement.

- At the completion of the contract, a report to the contracting officer and the SBA, signed by an authorized official of each joint venture, explaining how and certifying that the performance of work requirements were met for the contract, and further certifying that the contract was performed in accordance with the appropriate required provisions for joint venture agreements.

A couple nuances are worthy of note. First for 8(a) contracts, the annual certification requirement will be part of the 8(a) annual report for the 8(a) Managing Venturer (and any other 8(a) joint venture members). Second, for whatever reason, for 8(a) contracts, the regulations require only the "performance of work" piece of the second bullet above and do not require a certification that the contract was performed in accordance with 13 C.F.R. § 124.513(c).

INSPECTION OF RECORDS

If you're planning a joint venture, be aware that the SBA could come knocking on the door. The SBA's regulations state that the joint venture partners "must allow SBA's authorized representatives, including representatives authorized by the SBA Inspector General, during normal business hours, access to its files to inspect and copy all records and documents related to the joint venture."

The odds of the SBA showing up on your doorstep are probably rather slim—but it could happen. It's a good idea to keep joint venture files and records in a segregated location just in case: that way, if the SBA does show up, everything the SBA should need is ready to go.

CHECK IT OUT: REGULATIONS DISCUSSED IN THIS PART
13 C.F.R. § 125.6 (Limitations on Subcontracting)
13 C.F.R. § 124.513 (8(a) Joint Ventures)
13 C.F.R. § 125.8 (Small Business Joint Ventures)
13 C.F.R. § 125.18 (SDVOSB & VOSB Joint Ventures)
13 C.F.R. § 126.616 (HUBZone Joint Ventures)
13 C.F.R. § 127.506 (WOSB & EDWOSB Joint Ventures)

ACRONYMS ARE FUN:
JV ACRONYM LIST

Federal government contracting is full of acronyms—and so is this Handbook. Please find below definitions for some of the acronyms you may encounter reading this Handbook.

8(a). A company participating in the SBA's 8(a) Business Development Program. 8(a)s can be awarded set-aside and sole source contracts.

CAGE. A Commercial and Government Entity code. A unique identifier assigned to a government contractor. Needed to register a JV in SAM.

CTA. A Contractor Team Arrangement. In the FAR, may refer to either a prime/subcontractor team or a JV. A GSA CTA is a special vehicle to pursue GSA Schedule orders.

DUNS. Data Universal Number System. An identifying number obtained from Dun & Bradstreet. Needed to register a JV in SAM.

EIN. An Employee Identification Number, obtained from the IRS. Needed to register a JV in SAM.

FAR. The Federal Acquisition Regulation. The FAR contains many of the regulations applicable to federal contracting—although most joint venture regulations aren't in the FAR.

GSA. The U.S. General Services Administration. GSA Schedule holders can form CTAs.

HUBZone. A company participating in the SBA's Historically Underutilized Business Zones program. HUBZones can be awarded set-aside and sole source contracts.

JV. A joint venture. The subject of this Handbook.

LLC. A limited liability company. Many government contracts JVs are formed as LLCs.

NAICS. The North American Industry Classification System. Most federal procurements are assigned a single, six-digit NAICS code with a corresponding size standard.

OHA. The SBA's Office of Hearings and Appeals. Administrative judges who make final SBA decisions regarding various size and eligibility matters.

PTAC. A Procurement Technical Assistance Center. Provides free counseling to government contractors. Visit www.aptac-us.org to find the closest PTAC.

SAM. The System for Award Management (www.sam.gov). A joint venture must be registered in SAM.

SBA. The United States Small Business Administration. The SBA writes most of the regulations that govern joint venturing on federal contracts. The SBA must approve a joint venture before the JV can be awarded an 8(a) contract.

SDVOSB. A service-disabled, veteran-owned small business. SDVOSBs can be awarded set-aside and sole source contracts.

VA. The United States Department of Veterans Affairs. The VA must "verify" a joint venture before the joint venture can bid upon a VA SDVOSB or VOSB contract.

VOSB. A veteran-owned small business. VOSBs can be awarded set-aside and sole source contracts, but only by the VA.

WHIP. Walks and Hits per Innings Pitched. Often seen as a more meaningful measure of a pitcher's effectiveness than Earned Run Average (ERA). Unrelated to government contracts.

WOSB. A woman-owned small business. WOSBs can be awarded set-aside and sole source contracts.

INDEX

8(a) Program, 13, 14, 17, 25, 26, 29, 78
   prior approval, 63
   regulations, 61

affiliation, 35, 37, 38
All Small Mentor-Protégé Program, 25
   history, 26
amendments, 62
annual report, 76

CAGE code, 13, 43, 78
Center for Verification and Evaluation, 62
certifications, 13, 15, 67, 75
   8(a), 76
   8(a) joint venture, 75
   qualifications, 31
contract performance, 56
Contractor Team Arrangements (CTAs), 20, 78

DUNS numbers, 13, 43, 78

economically disadvantaged women owned small business (EDWOSB), 17, 29
ensured performance, 57
equipment, facilities and resources, 54, 55

Federal Acquisition Regulation (FAR), 6, 9, 78
Federal Supply Schedule (FSS), 19

government-wide acquisition contract (GWAC), 19

HUBZone, 13, 14, 17, 29, 79

indefinite delivery, indefinite quantity (IDIQ), 20, 54, 55
internal work split, 15

joint venture, 1, 6, 7, 10, 17, 18, 20, 27, 70, 79
    8(a) Program, 62, 64
    compliance, 68
    HUBZone, 31
    IDIQ, 20
    mentor protege, 26
    misconception, 62
    partnership, 44
    qualifications, 29, 30
    requirement, 72
    rules, 28, 67
    set-aside, 25, 46, 67
    size, 22
    template, 53
    three-in-two rule, 33
    verification, 64
    WOSB, 68
joint venture agreement, 11, 14, 26, 41, 44, 49
    8(a) Program, 62
    amendment, 61
    certification, 75
    compliance, 56
    documentation, 41
    generic, 61, 62
    regulations, 49
    requirements, 54, 57
    rules, 55
    WOSB, 75

limitations on subcontracting, 15, 69
limited liability company (LLC), 41, 44, 45, 59, 79
    joint ventures, 42

managing venturer, 50, 51, 52, 55, 56, 57, 60, 70, 73

reporting, 76
master teaming agreements, 18
mentor protégé, 10, 14, 24
    history, 26
    rules, 28
    set-aside, 47
mentor-protégé agreement, 11
multiple award contract (MAC), 19

NAICS code, 17, 22, 26, 68, 79
negotiation of the contract, 55
novation, 20

Office of Hearings and Appeals (OHA), 35, 79
operating agreement, 14, 41, 42
ostensible subcontractor affiliation, 10

partner venturer, 9, 55
past performance, 9
performance of work, 15, 56, 67, 75, 76
populated joint venture, 13
prime contract(ors), 7, 8, 10, 11, 15, 21, 24, 67, 68, 70
prior approval, 14, 62
profits, 52, 53
project manager, 50, 51, 56
PTAC, 43, 79

qualifications, 12, 17, 18

recordkeeping, 15, 58

Secretary of State, 11, 13
separate legal entity, 13, 40, 44, 45, 53
service disabled veteran owned small business (SDVOSB), 13, 14, 17, 29, 62, 79, 80
set-aside, 14, 17, 22, 23, 24, 29, 30, 59
    8(a) Program, 47

HUBZone, 48
SDVOSB, 47
socioeconomic, 74
WOSB, 48, 59
size appeal, 37
size eligibility, 12
size requirements, 11, 12, 17, 23
Small Business Administration (SBA), 6, 9, 11, 12, 14, 15, 18, 25, 26, 61, 68
   8(a) Program, 64
   approval, 64
   regulations, 36, 40, 45, 52, 74, 77
   restrictions, 45
   rules, 23, 31
   three-in-two rule, 32
socioeconomic eligibility, 13, 17, 29, 31
source of labor, 55
special bank account, 53
subcontract(ors), 7, 8, 10, 11, 12, 21, 24
System for Award Management (SAM), 11, 13, 43, 79

teaming agreements, 11
templates, 49, 53
termination, 10, 11
three-in-two rule, 12, 18, 32, 62
   affiliation, 35
   history, 32
   restrictions, 33, 35

unpopulated joint venture, 13, 45
   restriction, 45

woman owned small business (WOSB), 80
women owned small business (WOSB), 13, 14, 17, 29, 59
   set-aside, 30

BIOS

Steven J. Koprince is the founder and Managing Partner of Koprince Law LLC, where his practice focuses exclusively on providing comprehensive legal services to federal government contractors. He is the author of *The Small-Business Guide to Government Contracts* (AMACOM Books, 2012) and founded the blog *SmallGovCon* (smallgovcon.com), where he has written nearly 1,000 posts on contracting issues. Steven has been quoted in several national news outlets, has appeared on numerous radio programs and podcasts, and has spoken to audiences across the country on government contracting and small business matters.

Steven is a graduate of Duke University and the Marshall-Wythe School of Law at the College of William & Mary. He lives in Lawrence, Kansas, with his wife and two children.

Steven can be reached by email at skoprince@koprince.com or by phone at (785) 200-8919. He welcomes readers to follow him on Twitter (@stevenkoprince) and connect with him on LinkedIn.

Candace Shields is a Senior Associate Attorney with Koprince Law LLC. Candace's legal practice focuses on federal government contract law. Candace regularly drafts and negotiates joint venture agreements for federal government contractors. She gained experience as an Attorney Advisor at the U.S. Social Security Administration in the Washington, D.C. area before joining the team at Koprince Law in the summer of 2016. Candace is a regular contributor on the blog SmallGovCon (smallgovcon.com) and recently coauthored an article in *The Procurement Lawyer*.

Candace is a graduate of University of Michigan and earned her law degree at The Catholic University of America, Columbus School of Law. She resides in Lawrence, Kansas with her husband and two children.

Koprince Law LLC

When government contracting is the lifeblood of your business, you owe it to yourself to work with attorneys who understand the government's complex rules, regulations, and processes for its contractors.

Koprince Law provides comprehensive legal solutions to government contractors. Period. We don't pretend to be everything to everyone. Instead we think it makes sense to focus on being very good at one thing – government contracts law.

Contact us:

(785) 200-8919   www.koprince.com   info@koprince.com

SMALLGOVCON

SmallGovCon is a blog providing legal news, notes and commentary of interest to small government contractors. Written in plain English by the government contracts attorneys of Koprince Law LLC, SmallGovCon covers regulatory updates, bid protests, size appeals, federal court decisions and much more. Visit smallgovcon.com to check out our posts and sign up for our free monthly electronic newsletter.

Made in the USA
Middletown, DE
26 December 2019